Dr. Seuss's HORSE MUSEUM

illustrated by Andrew Joyner

Random House New York

ART.

What's it all about?

This is what ART is about...

ART is when an artist looks at something...

...like a horse, for instance...

...and they see something in that horse that excites them...

So they do something about it.

They tell you about it...

...in any one of a number of ways.

Artists have been excited by horses for as long as there have been artists. But *what* an artist tells us about horses and *how* they tell us is different for every artist.

What an artist sees in a horse depends on many different things— their background, likes and dislikes, you name it.

So come with me...

Let's look at how different artists have seen horses. Maybe we can find some new ways of looking at them ourselves?

Look it over.
Think it over.
Talk it over.

When most people look at me,
they *just see me* like this.

BUT...

. . . when an artist looks at me,
they see a million other things.

Can you?

Axes, Susan Rothenberg

Lintel,
from Roquepertuse,
France

Some artists look at a horse
and see its *OUTLINES.*

To other artists, like this
Chinese sculptor, a horse is
not an outline at all. A horse
is *BULK,* a *SOLID FORM.*

Harnessed horse,
northern Wei dynasty

19

A Japanese artist
looked at a horse.
What he saw was
BEAUTIFUL LINES.
Beautiful lines from
head to tail.

Studies of Horses, Katsushika Hokusai

Bedouins on Horseback (Racing), Mané-Katz

Some artists look at a horse and find *COLOR*.

Study for **Sussex Farm Horse,** Robert Polhill Bevan

Other artists are interested in *SHAPE.*

24

Cavallo, Marino Marini

This artist looked at a horse
and saw **STRENGTH.**

Horses Straining at a Load, Charles Verlat

The Horse in Motion, Eadweard Muybridge

These artists looked and they saw *SPEED*.

The Derby at Epsom, Théodore Géricault

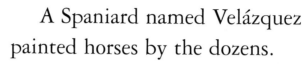

A Spaniard named Velázquez painted horses by the dozens.

He saw them as something for kings and princes to sit on while he painted them.

(Velázquez worked for the kings and princes. He never got any money from the horses.)

Gaspar de Guzmán,
Count-Duke of Olivares,
Diego Velázquez

1807, **Friedland,** Ernest Meissonier

32

This painting is by
a Frenchman named
Meissonier.

Horses to him were
something necessary
to carry generals into
battle. He loved to
paint generals going
into battle.

To him the horse
was a Jeep, in the days
before the Jeep was
invented.

Chinese Horse, Lascaux cave

On the rock walls of a cave in France nearly 22,000 years ago, someone painted this horse by the light of a fire.

What did the cave artist see in a horse?

We don't know. It's a mystery.

What do YOU think?

Two thousand years ago in Greece, artists looked at horses and imagined them with wings.

Pegasus was an immortal flying horse in Greek mythology.

Jug,
White Sakkos
Painter

Greek artists painted horses with wings as *symbols* for ideas—like immortality—that are hard to show in a picture.

The Game of Polo, illustration from the Book of Kings

Five hundred years ago in Persia, people thought *a horse was for having fun on.*

And that's what the Persian artists saw when they looked at horses.

Saint George Fighting the Dragon, Raphael

Five hundred years ago in Italy, the artist Raphael looked at a horse. He thought that *a horse was for fighting dragons on.*

Two Horses in a Paddock,
George Stubbs

The Horse Fair, Rosa Bonheur

Of course, some artists looked at horses and wanted to paint them just as they appeared in the natural world. Doing things that horses really do.

We call this kind of art realistic.

At the Races, Edouard Manet

The Harnessed Horse, Georges Seurat

Other artists looked at horses and tried to capture them in a moment of time. We call this style of art **Impressionism.** Impressionist art often has a soft, slightly out-of-focus appearance.

Then we come to what people call modern art.

Some people call this "crazy stuff."

Maybe they're right. Maybe they're wrong.

But these ARE paintings, drawings, and sculptures that show what certain artists imagined when they looked at a horse.

So please look at them very carefully.

There are lots of ways of looking at things.

Maybe these pictures have something to tell you.

43

Surrealism is a way of looking at things—including horses—that draws on, in part, an artist's dreams.

Dreams can be very strange—and so can surrealist art.

Marine Rutting, Óscar Domínguez

The Lost Jockey, René Magritte

Man with a Horse on his Head, Lucian Freud

Horse Team, Edvard Munch

Expressionism is an art style that uses exaggerated colors and brushstrokes to show the *emotion* an artist wants us to feel when we look at something.

Blue Horse I, Franz Marc

What do YOU feel when you look at this?

Cubism is a way of looking at things from different angles all at the same time. Cubists don't want to copy things the way they normally look.

48

Horse's Head, study for **Guernica,** Pablo Picasso

A famous artist named Picasso liked horses. He liked bulls, too. He drew a lot of them.

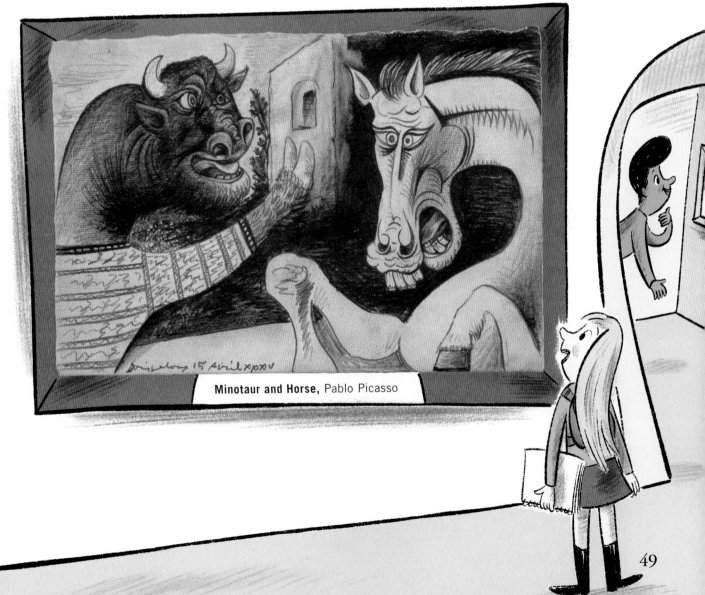

Minotaur and Horse, Pablo Picasso

49

The Life of Toussaint L'Ouverture #34, Jacob Lawrence

Abstract art can have a subject—but it doesn't NEED one! It uses color and shape to create a visual experience. (These abstract images DO have subjects—horses and riders, of course.)

50

Lyrical, Vasily Kandinsky

This artist used just
a few lines and splotches
of color in this woodcut.
But when you look at it,
you can see a galloping
horse and rider, right?

What do YOU see when you look at branches and driftwood? The artist who made this sculpture saw a horse.

Untitled (bark),
Deborah Butterfield

This abstract "drawing in space" shows what LOOKS like a big, strong horse. But you wouldn't want to sit on its back. All it is made of is thin steel wire.

(Ouch!)

Horse, Alexander Calder

An American painter named Jackson Pollock found a hobbyhorse head and glued it onto a canvas before doing this abstract "drip painting."

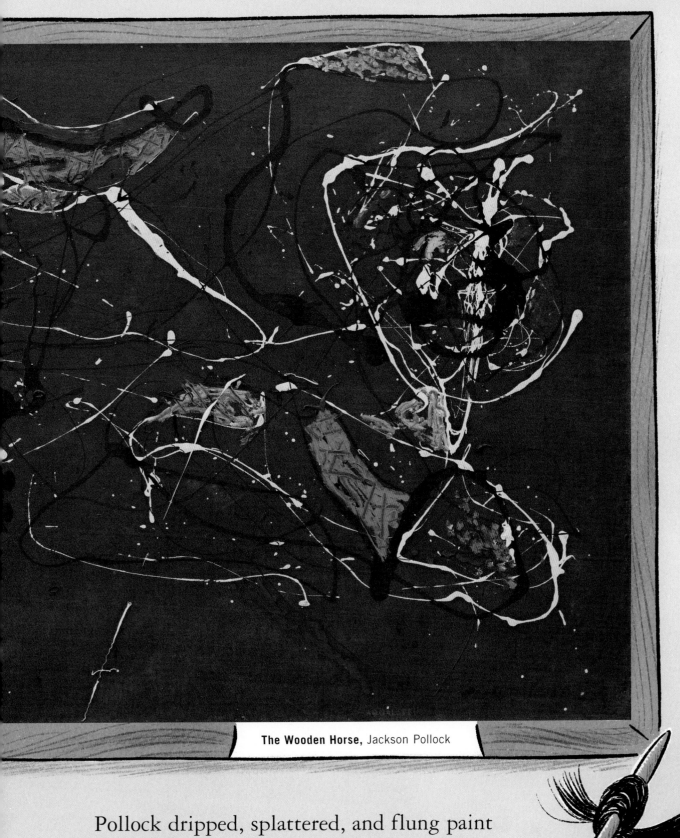

The Wooden Horse, Jackson Pollock

Pollock dripped, splattered, and flung paint
as a way to insert himself INTO his paintings.
Maybe this is Pollock ON a horse?

So what do YOU think? Is this stuff crazy? Or is it CRAZY GOOD?

Looking at art—and thinking about it—is fun. There's no right or wrong way to do it. Museums are good places to find art. You can find art in other places, too.

One such place to look is in books. The horses shown below and to the right are from books illustrated by a man who never studied drawing. His name was Dr. Seuss.

Dr. Seuss didn't ride horses, but he looked at them carefully and saw something in them. Can you guess what that something was?

YERTLE THE TURTLE
HAPPY BIRTHDAY TO YOU!
THE FOOT BOOK
THE LORAX
SCRAMBLED EGGS SUPER
ONE FISH TWO FISH RED FISH BLUE FISH
HOP ON POP
OH, THE PLACES YOU'LL GO!
HOW THE GRINCH STOLE CHRISTMAS
GREEN EGGS AND HAM
THE SNEETCHES
IF I RAN THE ZOO
FOX IN SOCKS
HORTON HEARS A WHO

THE CAT IN THE HAT

So . . . *look at that horse once again.*
A horse is many, many, many things.
All depending on what **YOU** see.

And the shape
of smoke
and
marshmallows
and
fires.

And mountains

and

roosters

and

horses

and

tires!

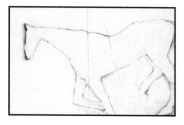

Susan Rothenberg, *Axes,* 1976, synthetic polymer paint, gesso, charcoal, and pencil on canvas.

American artist Susan Rothenberg became known in the 1970s for a series of paintings showing the outlines of horses. She took riding lessons as a child, but does not consider herself a horse fancier. As a young artist, she discovered she needed to paint something "physically relating to this world. . . . The horse was a way of not doing people, yet it was a symbol of people, a self-portrait, really."

Lintel with a relief depicting horses' heads, from Roquepertuse, France, 4th–3rd century BC, stone.

Roquepertuse is a prehistoric site in southern France, believed to have been used as a religious center by the Celts. Horses were essential to all areas of Celtic life, and the animals were revered, taking on a religious significance. Images of horses can be found in Celtic art throughout the centuries.

Harnessed horse, northern Wei dynasty, AD 386–535, terra-cotta.

Thought to be related to dragons, horses were a symbol of power and status in ancient China. Terra-cotta (clay) statues like this one from the northern Wei dynasty were often placed in tombs for use in the afterlife. In fact, 670 terra-cotta horses—and 8,000 terra-cotta soldiers—were buried in the tomb belonging to Emperor Qin Shi Huang, the First Emperor of China.

Katsushika Hokusai, *Studies of Horses,* c. 1815–1849, ink on paper.

From the age of five, Japanese artist Katsushika Hokusai said he "had a mania for sketching the form of things." He would produce over 30,000 works. Late in his life, he described himself as an "old man mad with painting." His last words were said to be "If only heaven will give me just another 10 years . . . then I could become a *real* painter."

Mané-Katz, *Bedouins on Horseback (Racing),* c. 1950–1959, oil on canvas.

Born in Ukraine into an Orthodox Jewish family, Mané-Katz's father had hoped he would become a rabbi. Instead, he moved to Paris at nineteen to study art. He would become known for his painting of village life in the shtetls of Eastern Europe. Horses—including Arab riders, circus horses, mares with foals, and horses engaged in bullfighting scenes—are a recurring theme in his work.

Robert Polhill Bevan, Study for *Sussex Farm Horse*, c. 1904–1906, oil on canvas.

Growing up in the English countryside, Robert Bevan had two passions: painting and horses. As the son of a wealthy banker, he was free to indulge both. He studied painting and was encouraged to exploit his love of horses in his art. At his first solo exhibition, critics found his use of strong color shocking. Today he is considered one of the first English artists to use "pure color" in the twentieth century.

***Oh, My Beautiful Horses,* Navajo Pictorial Blanket, 1885–1900, Lukachukai Mountain Weaving District, Arizona.**

The Navajo people of the Four Corners area of the United States are renowned for their fine textiles, which are traditionally woven by women. Most weavings feature geometrical designs. Pictorial blankets, like this one that shows horses, corn, and a woman, are less common. Horses, however, are a common theme for those blankets that are representational. According to legend, weaving was taught to the Navajo people by Spider Woman, a mythological figure who helped humans by teaching them survival skills.

Marino Marini, *Cavallo*, 1954, oil on board.

Italian artist Marino Marini is best-known for his equestrian paintings and sculptures. He used images of horses and riders as symbols. He is quoted as saying: "The entire history of humanity and nature can be found in the figure of the horse and rider, whatever the era. It is my way of narrating history."

Charles Verlat, *Horses Straining at a Load*, 1864, oil on canvas.

Horses, dogs, cats, birds, tigers, and buffalo are among the many animals painted by Belgian artist Charles Verlat—who also painted portraits and historical subjects. But he is perhaps best-known for his satirical paintings of monkeys dressed in clothing and behaving like humans.

Eadweard Muybridge, *The Horse in Motion*, Animal Locomotion series, c. 1878, black-and-white photograph.

Does a galloping horse ever have all four feet off the ground? That was the question British photographer Eadweard Muybridge set out to prove when creating *The Horse in Motion.* Using twelve cameras placed along a racetrack, he invented a way to take photos in fast succession as a horse ran past. (The horse tripped wires attached to the cameras.) The subject of the resulting images was the *motion* of the horse.

Théodore Géricault, *The Derby at Epsom,* 1821, oil on canvas.
French artist Théodore Géricault loved horses and began sketching them as a child. His mother died when he was seventeen, leaving him an inheritance that made him independently wealthy and free to pursue his two passions: horses and art. He became an accomplished rider and a largely self-taught painter, destined for greatness before his untimely death at thirty-two—from a condition made worse by a fall from a horse.

Diego Velázquez, *Gaspar de Guzmán, Count-Duke of Olivares,* 1635, oil on canvas.
Official painter to King Philip IV of Spain, Velázquez painted this portrait of Guzmán—a skilled politician who worked closely with the king. The painting shows Guzmán effortlessly handling an idealized horse who stands up on his back legs. Do you think Guzmán could really handle a horse like that? Maybe. Maybe not. But he certainly looks like a powerful politician.

Ernest Meissonier, *1807, Friedland,* c. 1861–1875, oil on canvas.
French artist Ernest Meissonier is best known for his paintings of historical and military subjects, often featuring Napoléon Bonaparte. He paid extraordinary attention to historical accuracy and detail in his work, often spending years on a single painting. *1807, Friedland* took him *fifteen* years to complete. The painting was sold *sight unseen* in 1876 for $60,000—an astronomical sum, well over a million dollars today.

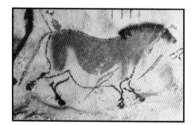

Chinese Horse, prehistoric cave painting, Lascaux cave, Dordogne, France, c. 16,950–16,650 BC.
Discovered by four boys and their dog in 1940, Lascaux is a series of caves in southwest France famous for its paintings, which are estimated to be up to 20,000 years old. Almost all the images are of animals once native to the region, with horses being the most common. The Chinese Horse is in a part of the cave that has been called the Sistine Chapel of Prehistory.

White Sakkos Painter, Jug with depiction of Pegasus, Apulia, c. 310 BC.
The name of the artist who painted this jug is unknown. Scholars, however, have found many pieces of ceramics that appear to have been painted by the same artist, and they've given that artist the name White Sakkos Painter.

The Game of Polo, illustration (c. 1500s) from the *Shahnama (Book of Kings),* by Abu'l-Qasim Manur Firdawsi (c. 934–1020).

Arguably the oldest team sport in recorded history, polo was first played in Persia (modern Iran) between 600 BC and AD 100. It was played by the nobility and military. This miniature painting comes from a famous book about the history of Iran. The pigments used to create miniature paintings like this came from crushed minerals, insects, and even cow urine.

Raphael, *Saint George Fighting the Dragon,* c. 1505, oil on wood.
Italian artist Raphael—one of the masters of the High Renaissance—painted two different images of Saint George fighting the dragon. Many other artists from around the world have also depicted this legend. In it, Saint George is shown on a white horse, a symbol of goodness, slaying a dragon, a symbol of evil.

George Stubbs, *Two Horses in a Paddock,* 1788, oil painting on panel.
George Stubbs was always fascinated with anatomy. His father was a tanner, and George helped him prepare hides. Largely self-taught, Stubbs was apprenticed to study painting but quit after a few weeks. He objected to the teacher's methods and wanted to learn by studying nature.

Before he began to paint horses, Stubbs undertook an eighteen-month-long study of horse anatomy. After acquiring horses from a slaughterhouse, he carefully dissected them, drawing each layer of their anatomy. His images were published in a groundbreaking book that is still in print. Stubbs then turned his attention to painting amazingly realistic portraits of live horses. He is considered one of the greatest horse painters of all time.

Rosa Bonheur, *The Horse Fair,* c. 1853–1855, oil on canvas.
Rosa Bonheur loved animals, and as a child, she kept many pets. Rosa began training as an artist at age thirteen, under the direction of her father. Bonheur closely observed her animal subjects. To prepare for painting *The Horse Fair,* she visited a horse market in Paris twice a week for a year and a half. To avoid drawing attention to herself while she sketched, she obtained permission from the police to dress as a man (which was illegal at the time). Her monumental finished painting—eight feet tall by sixteen feet wide—received international acclaim and was eventually bought by the same collector who owned Ernest Meissonier's *1807, Friedland.*

Edouard Manet, *At the Races,* c. 1875, oil on wood.
During his lifetime, French artist Edouard Manet was often criticized for his unique painting technique and the controversial subjects of his paintings. He rejected the classical tradition of building layers of paint on a canvas. Instead of layers, he used loose brushstrokes of color side by side to create the impression of light. Today he is considered by many to be the father of modern art.

Georges Seurat, *The Harnessed Horse,* 1883, oil on canvas.
This painting of a horse and cart was created using overlapping dots and strokes of color in a technique called Pointillism. Invented by Georges Seurat, Pointillism was based on scientific ideas about how the human eye sees color. By having different-colored dots of paint touch each other on the canvas, Seurat believed the eye would mix them into a new color more vivid than if he mixed them on his pallet and then applied them to the canvas.

Óscar Domínguez, *Marine Rutting,* 1935, oil on canvas.
From childhood, surrealist painter Óscar Domínguez suffered from a severe illness that slowed his growth and disfigured his limbs and face. In *Marine Rutting,* Domínguez painted two horses: one with two heads (weighted down with anchors), and one with two tails. Could the artist's own disfigurement have influenced his painting?

René Magritte, *The Lost Jockey,* 1926, collage, gouache, watercolor, and pencil on paper.
Curtains and the image of a jockey riding though a strange environment were both recurring themes in the work of Belgian artist René Magritte. To support himself, Magritte designed books, wallpaper, and advertisements. He also designed theater sets, and the curtain in this collage, as in many of his works, makes the jockey appear to be onstage. The result is delightfully strange—and a bit disturbing. To quote Magritte, he was trying to "challenge the real world" in his art.

Lucian Freud, *Man with a Horse on His Head,* 1939, ink, pencil, and gouache on paper.
When seventeen-year old Lucian Freud (grandson of Sigmund Freud) drew this picture, he probably *did* have horses on his mind. Born in Berlin, his family had moved to London in 1933 to escape the Nazis. He spoke little English, and at his first boarding school spent much of his time taking care of the school's horses and learning to ride. In fact, he sometimes slept in the stables and at one point considered becoming a jockey. He would remain fascinated with horses—as well as dogs—for the rest of his life.

Edvard Munch, *Horse Team,* 1919, oil on canvas.

Norwegian artist Edvard Munch had a troubled childhood. Edvard was often ill, and he started drawing and painting to pass the time while he was home. Art was a way for him to make sense of life. Munch used color in a symbolic way. In *Horse Team,* a black horse and a white horse seem to pull away from each other as they work side by side. Could Munch have been saying something about the opposing forces of nature with these horses?

Franz Marc, *Blue Horse I,* 1911, oil on canvas.

German artist Franz Marc is famous for his boldly colored, dream-like paintings of animals, especially horses. To Marc, the horse was a spiritual creature connected to nature in a way that was lost to humanity. In his essay "How Does a Horse See the World?" Marc wrote, "Is there a more mysterious idea for an artist than to imagine how nature is reflected in the eyes of an animal? How does a horse see the world, how does an eagle, a doe, or a dog?"

Pablo Picasso, *Horse's Head,* study for *Guernica,* 1937, oil on canvas.

Horses appear over and over in Spanish artist Pablo Picasso's work, in drawings, paintings, engravings, ceramics, costumes, and even paper cutouts. In fact, his first oil painting—done when he was eight—is of a man on a horse. *Horse's Head* is a study, or practice piece, created by Picasso for his famous painting *Guernica,* which shows the horrors of war. Although credited with co-founding Cubism, Picasso created artworks in many different styles.

Pablo Picasso, *Minotaur and Horse,* 1935, lead pencil.

Along with the horse, the minotaur (a mythological creature that is half man and half bull) was a frequent subject of Picasso's art. In fact, Picasso kept a bull mask in his studio, which he would sometimes wear on his head. Could the bull in this painting *be* Picasso? Maybe. Maybe not. Picasso felt it was up to the viewer to interpret his art.

Jacob Lawrence, *The Life of Toussaint L'Ouverture #34,* 1938, tempera on paper.

Jacob Lawrence learned to draw and paint as a boy in an after-school arts program held in his Harlem neighborhood. At twenty-one, he completed a series of forty-one paintings narrating the story of Toussaint L'Ouverture—the former slave who became a leader of the Haitian Revolution. Lawrence wrote captions for each painting. He called his graphic style of painting "dynamic cubism," and he went on to create narrative series about Frederick Douglass, Harriet Tubman, John Brown, and African American experiences.

Vasily Kandinsky, *Lyrical,* 1913, woodcut from an illustrated book.

Lyrical is one of fifty-six woodcuts by Vasily Kandinsky that illustrate a book of poetry that he wrote. Using just a few lines, the image shows a horse and rider—a symbol that appears throughout Kandinsky's work. He used it to represent a break from conventional values and to suggest a more spiritual future. Born in Russia, Kandinsky studied law and economics at the University of Moscow. After receiving his degree and teaching law, he began studying to become a painter. He is often credited with creating the first abstract painting (which he named *First Abstract Watercolor)* in 1910.

Deborah Butterfield, *Untitled (bark),* 1994, bronze.

Deborah Butterfield's first memories are of horses. Born in California, she grew up riding—and still does so today, competing in dressage. She began sculpting horses in college, and they are the single subject of her work. Butterfield "draws" her horses with found objects, including branches, scrap metal, barbed wire, pipes, and fencing, which she then casts in bronze. She has said, "I first used the horse images as a metaphorical substitute for myself—it was a way of doing a self-portrait one step removed from the specificity of Deborah Butterfield."

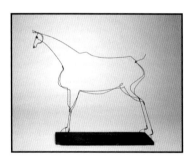

Alexander Calder, *Horse,* c. 1928, wire and wood.

American artist Alexander Calder first began working with wire when he was eight years old, making jewelry for his sister's dolls. As an adult, he began using wire to create portraits and figures that critics called "drawings in space." At first Calder's wire sculptures were figurative and stationary, like this horse. Eventually, Calder began making abstract sculptures out of sheet metal and wire that moved. First they moved by cranks or motors, and eventually, they moved all by themselves. In 1931, Marcel Duchamp called these kinetic sculptures "mobiles." Have you ever hung a mobile in your room? If so, say thanks to Alexander Calder!

Jackson Pollock, *The Wooden Horse,* 1948, oil, enamel, and wood hobbyhorse head on brown cotton canvas, mounted on fiberboard.

Born in Wyoming, Jackson Pollock was often mistaken for a cowboy. But he was actually afraid of horses. When he was five years old, he was riding with his mother in a horse-drawn buggy, when a bull charged their cart. Their horse reared in panic, and Jackson and his mother were thrown from the buggy. Pollock had nightmares about the event for the rest of his life.

Encouraged by his high school art teacher, Pollock moved to New York in 1930 to study art. He began to experiment with "drip painting" in 1947. Using a can of paint and tools like sticks, his hands, and even turkey basters, he dripped, poured, and flung paint at a canvas on the floor. Through these actions, Pollock was able to insert himself "into" his artwork. To quote Pollock himself: "Today painters do not have to go to a subject matter outside of themselves. Most modern painters work from a different source. They work from within. . . . The modern artist, it seems to me, is working and expressing an inner world."

Dr. Seuss, illustration from *Bartholomew and the Oobleck,* 1949.
The horses in Dr. Seuss books have at least one thing in common: they're all pretty funny. Dr. Seuss once said that "the trick is to imply with your illustrations what you're not allowed to say with words." In this illustration, the horse under King Derwin has its eyes rolled, as if it's thinking, "Oh, brother—what now?"

Dr. Seuss, illustration from *The Shape of Me and Other Stuff,* 1973.
The Shape of Me is unique among Dr. Seuss books in that it's illustrated entirely with silhouettes. Dr. Seuss was inspired by some photographs he saw in a magazine. The photos were of stone silhouettes carved by the Inuit people of Quebec. He said the silhouettes were "among the strongest illustrations I've ever seen."

Dr. Seuss's HORSE MUSEUM

NOTES FROM THE PUBLISHER

According to his wife Audrey, Ted Geisel (aka Dr. Seuss) had no interest in horses. But something that definitely *did* interest him was art. It had been that way all his life.

Ted began drawing as a young child. He kept pencils near his bed for doodling (on paper and on the walls), and he carried a sketchbook with him on weekends when he'd visit the zoo in Springfield, Massachusetts. Ted drew animals his own way—with exaggerated and mismatched features. He said he viewed the world "through the wrong end of the telescope."

In high school, Ted took his first—and only—art class. He was sketching a still life and had turned his drawing pad upside down to work on when the teacher stopped him. "No, Theodor. Not upside down. There are rules that every artist must abide by." Ted transferred out after that one class. He had a natural understanding of how to draw and didn't believe in art "by the rule books."

In college at Dartmouth, Ted studied English literature and writing. Later, with no formal training, Ted would go on to make his living as an artist: as a cartoonist, an advertising artist, a sculptor, and eventually as the very successful author and illustrator of forty-two children's books.

But that didn't mean Ted wasn't interested in *learning* about art. He traveled widely and visited museums around the world. He spoke to educators and other artists about art. He became a trustee of the San Diego Museum of Fine Arts. And, as his wife Audrey discovered in 2013, he wrote a book about art, too.

Twenty-one years after Ted's death, Audrey Geisel was cleaning out Ted's studio and found a box containing a manuscript and sketches for a book titled *Horse Museum.* The book you are reading now is based on that manuscript and those sketches.

Horse Museum was found in the same box that also included Ted's manuscript and sketches for *What Pet Should I Get?,* which Random House published in 2015. Neither manuscript was dated. We can only guess when *Horse Museum* was written—we suspect it was the early 1950s.

It was around this time that Ted wrote a script for a half-hour educational television show about modern art. Titled *Modern Art on Horseback,* the program starred Ted (as Dr. Seuss), the actors Burgess Meredith, Hans Conried, and Dorothy Donahue; six students from the Cooper Union School of Art; and a white stallion. The premise of the show: When a modern artist paints a picture of a horse, why doesn't the horse look like a horse?

Before the broadcast, Ted spent ten days with the art students discussing ideas about painting. Then each student actor received a script written by Ted, which they were to follow. Here is an excerpt:

> When an artist looks at a horse, the image of that horse goes into his brain. And there, in the brain, is where the artistry takes place. . . . [The artist] looks at it . . . NOT from a photographic point of view. He says to himself . . . what does this horse mean to me, personally?
>
> What any artist sees in a horse depends entirely on that artist's background . . . his education . . . his experience . . . his likes and dislikes and a thousand other things. To one artist a horse may mean speed . . . to another, strength . . . to another gentleness. . . . Another artist can look at this horse and only see color or some beautiful lines . . . or some interesting shapes.

Sadly, film footage of the television program no longer exits. But Cooper Union published a copy of the television script, and a photograph from that publication is shown at right. And for whatever reason, Ted's manuscript and sketches for *Horse Museum* were placed in a box with *What Pet Should I Get?*

About three-quarters of the *Horse Museum* text was in the box. What was missing from the manuscript were pages on modern art (whose artists Ted referred to as the Contemporaries). If you look at

the bottom-right corner of the sketch below, you'll see that Ted wrote: "Lead into examples of Surrealism, Expressionism, Cubism and Abstraction and non-objective art with explanations."

With the exception of the missing pages on modern art, Ted drew rough pencil sketches for the entire book. The unfinished manuscript and sketches are a priceless find of great interest to scholars and others who admire Dr. Seuss. But to reach Ted's intended audience of children, Dr. Seuss Enterprises and the editors at Random House decided to complete the missing sections of text (which they did themselves) and to hire an illustrator—Andrew Joyner—to bring the book to life.

Andrew lives in a small rural town in Australia, which (to quote Andrew) "could be described as horse-obsessed." In fact, his local high school offers a class in Equine Studies. But Andrew is not himself a horse enthusiast.

To draw the horses in this book, Andrew first looked at how Ted Geisel drew horses. He even gave himself an art lesson by copying some of Ted's horses. "But I can't draw like Ted. In fact, I'm not sure anyone can. Even his simplest sketches are instantly recognizable and distinctly his own. Ted's horses look nothing like my horses."

Andrew also looked at Ted's sketches for *Horse Museum.* "I sense an energy and spirit in them—an urge to communicate and connect with the young reader which is apparent in all of Ted's work. I hope there's some of this energy in my own illustrations." Following are some of Ted's original sketches for *Horse Museum* and Andrew's illustrations for those same pages. As you see, in the first example below, they're similar. In the second example (on the next page), they're very different. We think they capture Ted's energy. Do you?

Some artists look at a horse and find COLOR

Some artists look at a horse and find **COLOR**.

For *Horse Museum,* Andrew did all his drawing on an iPad Pro with an Apple Pencil. "What I like about drawing on the iPad is that there is no real gap between my sketches and the final art—it's all one continuous process. I tried to reference elements of Ted's sketches in my final art, for example, his use of colored pencil. And the color palette for the book was inspired by the verse from *Oh, the Thinks You Can Think!*:

> You can think up some birds.
> That's what you can do.
> You can think about yellow
> Or think about blue . . .
> You can think about red.
> You can think about pink.
> You can think up a horse.
> Oh, the THINKS you can think!

I see the bow-tied horse that guides us through the museum as a version of Ted and his unique way of seeing."

But the question remains: *Why horses?* While horses do make cameo appearances throughout Ted's books, the animal that seems to have most "spoken" to Ted's imagination throughout his life is the cat.

Ted had been drawing animals—including cats—since he was a child. But in 1957, a cat (*the* Cat) would star in a book that changed the course of his life, bringing him unimaginable professional success and considerable wealth—*The Cat in the Hat*. The Cat would continue to appear in Ted's books throughout his life: in *The Cat in the Hat Comes Back* (1958); *The Cat in the Hat Songbook* (1967); *I Can Lick 30 Tigers Today! And Other Stories* (1969); *The Cat's Quizzer* (1976); and *I Can Read with My Eyes Shut!* (1978).

But the Cat was not the only feline to appear in Ted's work. Cats appear in many of his books. In fact, they star in great quantity in one of Ted's earliest works: *The King's Stilts* (1939). The thousand Patrol Cats in *Stilts* are the largest and smartest cats in the world, and everything in the Kingdom of Binn depends on them. According to King Birtram, "They are more important than our army, our navy, and the fire department too."

Late at night, Ted liked to paint for his own personal pleasure. These "Midnight Paintings," as he called them, were not for public view. They hung in Ted's home. He didn't sell them, and they were rarely, if ever, exhibited. Wildly different in style than his children's book illustrations, these Midnight Paintings are *probably* best described as surrealist. (In a 1982 interview for the *Chicago Tribune,* Ted himself described his style as "fragmented modern.") In any case, these Midnight Paintings are otherworldly, uniquely Seussian, and littered with cats! Here are a few examples. See for yourself:

(Above) *Archbishop Katz* (1964)

(Top right) *Cat in Obsolete Shower Bath* (study) (undated)

(Bottom right) *Green Cat with Lights* (undated)

(Opposite page) *A Plethora of Cats* (1970) According to Ted's wife Audrey, there was never actually a moment when Ted felt finished adding cats to *A Plethora of Cats.* "He would periodically step back and put [the painting] aside for a while. Then, inevitably, when the spirit again moved him—or he was on book hiatus—he would find room for just one more cat face. This happened over and over again."

Ted's stepdaughter Lark Dimond-Cates once said she thought "the Cat [in the Hat] was Ted on his good days, and the Grinch was Ted on his bad days." Could cats appear throughout Ted's work as a kind of symbol for himself—as artist Deborah Butterfield's horses are a substitute for herself? Or could Ted have painted cats for some magical purpose, as the cave painters in Lascaux perhaps did with their horses? We'll never know. Maybe, like Théodore Géricault and his horses, Ted just really *liked* cats. Whatever his motivation, it seems safe to say that Ted looked at cats and saw *something* in them that was meaningful to him personally, just as other artists have looked at and seen something in horses for millennia.

As Ted wrote in *Horse Museum,* artists have been painting horses since well before the invention of written language. Humans have gone from hunting them for food to riding them for pleasure. Since the horse was domesticated about 5,000 years ago, empires have been built on its back. No other animal has had such a big impact on human history. For a man like Ted, who was compelled since childhood to draw animals, the allure of the horse to artists throughout time must have been obvious.

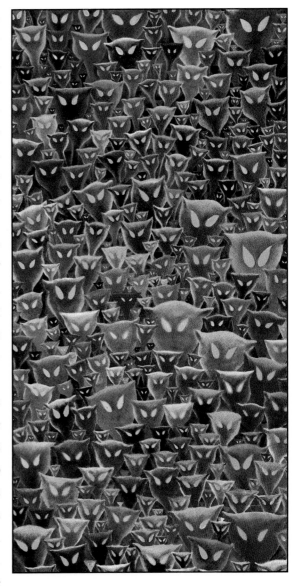

So next time you look at a work of art—whether it depicts a horse, an abstract design, or even a can of soup—remember Ted's advice:

Look it over. Think it over. Talk it over.

By doing so, you *may* learn a new way of looking at the world. Or not. And that's okay. Because at the heart of all Dr. Seuss books is the importance of thinking and seeing and embracing your unique self. A horse is many, many different things to different people. And so is art.

PICTURE CREDITS

p. 16: *Axes,* 1976 (synthetic polymer paint, gesso, charcoal, and pencil on canvas), Rothenberg, Susan (1945–) / The Museum of Modern Art, New York / Digital Image © The Museum of Modern Art / Licensed by SCALA / Art Resource, NY / © 2019 Susan Rothenberg / Artists Rights Society (ARS), NY

p. 17: Lintel with a relief depicting horses' heads, from Roqueperteuse, 4th–3rd century BC (stone), Gaulish / Musée de la Vieille Charité, Marseille, France / Bridgeman Images

p. 19: Harnessed horse, northern Wei dynasty (terra-cotta) / Musée Cernuschi, Paris, France / © DeA Picture Library / Art Resource, NY

p. 21: *Studies of Horses,* c. 1815–1849 (ink on paper), (attributed to) Katsushika Hokusai (1760–1849) / Seattle Art Museum, Washington / Eugene Fuller Memorial Collection (#39.179)

p. 22: *Bedouins on Horseback (Racing),* 1950–1959 (oil on canvas), Mané-Katz (1894–1962) / Private Collection / Photo © Christie's Images / Bridgeman Images

p. 23: Study for *Sussex Farm Horse,* c. 1904–1906 (oil on canvas), Bevan, Robert Polhill (1865–1925) / Private Collection / Photo © Christie's Images / Bridgeman Images

p. 24: *Oh, My Beautiful Horses,* Navajo Pictorial Blanket, Lukachukai Mountain Weaving District, Arizona, USA, c. 1885–1900 (wool) / Mingei International Museum / Art Resource, NY

p. 25: *Cavallo,* 1954 (oil on board), Marini, Marino (1901–1980) / Private Collection / Photo © Christie's Images / Bridgeman Images / © 2019 Artists Rights Society (ARS), New York / SIAE, Rome

p. 26: *Horses Straining at a Load,* 1864 (oil on canvas), Verlat, Charles (1824–1890) / Shipley Art Gallery, Gateshead, Tyne & Wear, UK / © Tyne & Wear Archives & Museums / Bridgeman Images

p. 28: *The Horse in Motion,* "Animal Locomotion" series, c. 1878 (b/w photo), Muybridge, Eadweard (1830–1904) / Private Collection / Prismatic Pictures / Bridgeman Images

p. 29: *The Derby at Epsom,* oil on canvas (1821), Géricault, Théodore (1791–1824) / Louvre (Museum), Paris, France / Erich Lessing / Art Resource, NY

p. 31: *Gaspar de Guzmán, Count-Duke of Olivares,* 1635 (oil on canvas), Velázquez, Diego Rodriguez (1599–1660) / Museo del Prado, Madrid, Spain / Image © Museo Nacional del Prado / Art Resource, NY

pp. 32–33: *1807, Friedland,* c. 1861–1875 (oil on canvas), Meissonier, Ernest (1815–1891) / The Metropolitan Museum of Art, New York / Image © The Metropolitan Museum of Art / Art Resource, NY

p. 34: *Chinese Horse,* prehistoric cave painting / Lascaux Caves, Périgord, Dordogne, France / Art Resource, NY

p. 35: Jug with depiction of Pegasus (winged horse), painted by the White Sakkos Painter, Apulia, c. 310 BCE / bpk Bildagentur / Skulpturensammlung, Staatliche Kunstsammlungen, Dresden, German / Photo: Elke Estel and Hans-Peter Klut / Art Resource, NY

p. 36: *The Game of Polo,* illustration from the *Shahnama* (*Book of Kings*), by Abu'l-Qasim Manur Firdawsi (c. 934–c. 1020) / Biblioteca Nazionale, Naples, Italy / Universal Images Group / Art Resource, NY

p. 37: *Saint George Fighting the Dragon,* c. 1505 (oil on wood), Raphael (Raffaello Sanzio) (1483–1520) / Louvre (Museum), Paris, France / © RMN-Grand Palais / Art Resource, NY

p. 38: *Two Horses in a Paddock,* 1788 (oil painting on panel), Stubbs, George (1724–1806) / Ascott, Buckinghamshire, Great Britain / National Trust Photo Library / Art Resource, NY

p. 39: *The Horse Fair,* 1853–1855 (oil on canvas), Bonheur, Rosa (1822–1899) / The Metropolitan Museum of Art, New York / Image © The Metropolitan Museum of Art / Image source: Art Resource, NY

p. 40: *At the Races,* c. 1875 (oil on wood), Manet, Edouard (1832–1883) / National Gallery of Art, Washington DC, USA / Bridgeman Images

p. 41: *The Harnessed Horse,* 1883 (oil on canvas), Seurat, Georges Pierre (1859–1891) / Solomon R. Guggenheim Museum, New York, USA / Bridgeman Images

p. 44: *Marine Rutting,* 1935 (oil on canvas), Domínguez, Óscar (1906–1958) / Private Collection / Bridgeman Images / © 2019 Artists Rights Society (ARS), New York / ADAGP, Paris

p. 45 top: *The Lost Jockey,* 1926 (collage, gouache, watercolor, and pencil on paper), Magritte, René (1898–1967) / Private Collection / Banque d'Images, ADAGP / Art Resource, NY / © 2019 C. Herscovici / Artists Rights Society (ARS), NY

p. 45 bottom: *Man with a Horse on His Head,* 1939 (ink, pencil, and gouache on paper), Freud, Lucian (1922–2011) / Private Collection / © The Lucian Freud Archive / Bridgeman Images

p. 46: *Horse Team,* 1919 (oil on canvas), Munch, Edvard (1863–1944) / Nasjonalgalleriet, Oslo, Norway / Photo © O. Vaering / Bridgeman Images / © 2019 Artists Rights Society (ARS), NY

p. 47: *Blue Horse I,* 1911 (oil on canvas), Marc, Franz (1880–1916) / HIP / Art Resource, NY

p. 49 top: *Horse's Head,* study for *Guernica,* 1937 (oil on canvas), Picasso, Pablo (1881–1973) / Museo Nacional Centro de Arte Reina Sofia, Madrid, Spain / Album / Art Resource, NY / © 2019 Estate of Pablo Picasso / Artists Rights Society (ARS), NY

p. 49 bottom: *Minotaur and Horse,* Boisgeloup, April 15, 1935 (lead pencil), Picasso, Pablo (1881–1973) / Photo: Gérard Blot / © RMN-Grand Palais / Art Resource, NY / © 2019 Estate of Pablo Picasso / Artists Rights Society (ARS), NY

p. 50: *The Life of Toussaint L'Ouverture #34,* 1938 (tempera on paper), Lawrence, Jacob (1917–2000) / Amistad Research Center, Tulane University, New Orleans / Photo: The Jacob and Gwendolyn Lawrence Foundation / Art Resource, NY / © 2019 The Jacob and Gwendolyn Knight Lawrence Foundation, Seattle / Artists Rights Society (ARS), NY

p. 51: *Lyrical* (*Lyrisches*) (plate, folio 9) from *Klänge* (*Sounds*) by Vasily Kandinsky (1913). Woodcut from an illustrated book with fifty-six woodcuts, Kandinsky, Vasily (1866–1944) / © ARS, NY / The Museum of Modern Art, New York / Digital Image © The Museum of Modern Art / Licensed by SCALA / Art Resource, NY

p. 52: Untitled (bark), Butterfield, Deborah (b. 1949) / Indianapolis Museum of Art at Newfields, USA / Alice and Kirk McKinney Fund / Bridgeman Images / © 2019 Deborah Butterfield / Licensed by VAGA at Artists Rights Society (ARS), NY

p. 53: *Horse,* c. 1928 (wire and wood), Calder, Alexander (1898–1976) / Calder Foundation, New York / Art Resource, NY / © 2019 Calder Foundation, New York / Artists Rights Society (ARS), NY

pp. 54–55: *The Wooden Horse,* 1948 (oil, enamel, and wood hobbyhorse head on brown cotton canvas, mounted on fiberboard), Pollock, Jackson (1912–1956) / Moderna Museet, Stockholm / © 2019 The Pollock-Krasner Foundation / Artists Rights Society (ARS), NY

Dr. Seuss Enterprises, L.P. and Random House Children's Books
would like to thank
DR. TERRY BARRETT,
Professor Emeritus, The Ohio State University,
for his assistance in the preparation of this book.

First Printing

Picture credits can be found on page 76.

Grateful acknowledgment is made to the following for permission to reprint previously published materials:
The Cooper Union Library: Photograph and excerpt from "Cooper Union Art School Publication Number One,"
copyright © The Cooper Union. Used by permission of The Cooper Union Library. All rights reserved.
Dr. Seuss Enterprises, L.P.: Images from *Bartholomew and the Oobleck,* TM & © 1949, renewed 1976 by Dr. Seuss Enterprises, L.P.;
The Shape of Me and Other Stuff, TM & © 1973 by Dr. Seuss Enterprises, L.P.; and
The Secret Art of Dr. Seuss, TM & © 1995 by Dr. Seuss Enterprises, L.P. Used by permission of Dr. Seuss Enterprises, L.P.
All rights reserved.

Visit us on the Web!
Seussville.com
rhcbooks.com

Educators and librarians, for a variety of teaching tools, visit us at
RHTeachersLibrarians.com

Library of Congress Cataloging-in-Publication Data is available upon request.
ISBN 978-0-399-55912-9 (trade) — ISBN 978-0-399-55913-6 (lib. bdg.)
MANUFACTURED IN CHINA
10 9 8 7 6 5 4 3 2 1
First Edition